About the book

There are 12 GCE AS Level (Year 12 or lower sixth mocks) Mathematics papers & answers in this book. These are 4 sets of papers 1 & 2 written as practice papers for GCE AS Level Mathematics Examinations. Papers are mainly focusing on Edexcel, AQA, OCR, OCR MEI examination boards. However, you may still use this book as a practice for other GCE AS Level examination boards as well as Edexcel.

These papers are written according to the new 2017 syllabus and questions are potential questions for the upcoming examinations.

All the questions in this book are written by the author and they are new questions written purely to help and experience the students to prepare and test themselves for the upcoming AS Level mathematics exam.

Answers are included in this book. If you need to check your solutions, I advise you to ask your school mathematics teacher or your private mathematics tutor to mark your answers.

There are 6 sections to this book A, B, C, D, E & F. Each section contains 2 papers. Both papers of each section are calculator papers.

GCE AS Level Mathematics Potential Exam Papers

AS Level Mathematics Potential Exam Papers

(Year 12 Mock Exams)

for Edexcel, AQA, OCR MEI & OCR syllabuses
AS Level (year 12) mock papers including answers

(can also be used as a revision guide for other exam boards)

By Dilan Wimalasena

Contents

Section A

GCE AS Level Mathematics

Pure Mathematics

Potential Paper 1A

Students must have Mathematical Formulae
and Statistical Tables, Calculator.

Calculator is allowed

Time allowed
2 hours
Total 100 marks

Write answers to 3 significant figures unless stated
otherwise

1. a) Find the first 4 terms, in ascending powers of x, of the binomial expansion of
$$(3 + kx)^8$$
where k is a non-zero constant.

Give each term in its simplest form.

(4 marks)

Given that the coefficient of x^3 in this expansion is 1,701,000

b) Find the value of k.

(3 marks)

(total 7 marks)

2. i) Simplify
$$\sqrt{20} - \frac{80}{\sqrt{5}}$$
Write your answer in the form $a\sqrt{5}$, where a is an integer to be found.

(2 marks)

ii) Solve the equation
$$5^{4x-1} = 125$$
write your answer as a rational number.

(3 marks)

(total 5 marks)

3. $f(x) = 2x^3 + ax^2 - 28x + b$

Given that $(x - 3)$ & $(2x + 1)$ are factors of $f(x)$.

i) Find the values of a & b.

(5 marks)

ii) Factorise $f(x)$ completely.

(3 marks)

iii) Hence, or otherwise sketch the curve $y = f(x)$. State clearly all the points of intersections with coordinate axes.

(2 marks)

(total 10 marks)

4. Find

$$\int \frac{2x^5 - 3}{6x^2} dx$$

writing your answer in its simplest form.

(4 marks)

5. A ball rolls horizontally across a field in a straight line with constant speed. Initially the ball is at the point $P(3i - 2j)m$ relative to a fixed point O. After 5 seconds the ball is at the point $Q(-12i + 8j)m$ relative to the fixed point O.

Using this model

a) Prove that the ball passes through O.

(2 marks)

b) Calculate the speed of the ball.

(3 marks)
(total 5 marks)

6. $f(x) = 4x^2 + 5x - 1$

i)   Sketch the graph of $y = f(x)$.

(2 marks)

The point $A(1,8)$ lies on the curve $y = f(x)$.

ii)   Find the gradient of the tangent to the curve at A.

(3 marks)

The point B with the x coordinate $1 + h$ also lies on the curve.

iii)   Find the gradient of the line AB, giving your answer in terms of h in its simplest form.

(3 marks)

iv)   Explain the relationship between your answers to parts i) & ii).

(1 mark)
(total 9 marks)

7. Solve the following inequalities.
   i) $3x + 4 \geq x - 1$

   (2 marks)

   ii) $x^2 - 2x - 3 > 0$

   (3 marks)

   iii) Both $3x + 4 \geq x - 1$ & $x^2 - 2x - 3 > 0$

   (2 marks)
   (total 7 marks)

8. The triangle ABC has area $140cm^2$.

   Given that the lengths AB & BC have lengths $18cm$ & $19cm$ respectively.

   Given also that the angle ABC is obtuse.

   Work out the perimeter of the triangle ABC.

   (5 marks)

9. The value of a car is modelled by the formula

   $$V = 21{,}500e^{-\alpha t} + \beta, t \geq 0, t \in \mathbb{R}$$

   where V is the value of the car in pounds, t is the age of the car in years, and α and β are positive constants.

   Given that the value of the car is £24,000 when new and £15,500 two years later.

   i)   Find the values of α & β.

   (5 marks)

   ii)   Find the age of the car, in years, when the value of the car is £5,000.

   Give your answer to 2 decimal places.

   (4 marks)
   (total 9 marks)

10. Prove, using algebra, that for all even numbers the expression

$$n^2 - 2n$$

is always divisible by 8.

(4 marks)

11. Solve the following equations.

i) $\sin 3\theta = \frac{-\sqrt{3}}{2}, 60° \le \theta \le 240°$

(4 marks)

ii) $6\cos^2\theta + 7\sin\theta - 8 = 0, \ 0 \le \theta \le 360°$

(6 marks)
(total 10 marks)

12. A circle has centre coordinates $C(6,10)$. The line $y = \frac{1}{2}x$ is a tangent to the circle at the point P.

i)   Work out the equation of the circle.

(6 marks)

The line with equation $y = \frac{1}{2}x + \alpha$, where α is a non-zero constant, is also a tangent to the circle.

ii)   Find the value of α.

(3 marks)
(total 9 marks)

13. Solve the following

i) $7^x = 70$, giving your answer to 3 significant figures,

(3 marks)

ii) $\log_3(x - 1) - \log_3 x = \log_3 4$

(3 marks)
(total 6 marks)

14. The curve C has equation

$$y = x^3 - 5x^2 - 8x + 4$$

Find

a) $\dfrac{dy}{dx}$

(2 marks)

b) the coordinates of the turning points of C.

(4 marks)

c) $\dfrac{d^2y}{dx^2}$

(2 marks)

d) Determine the nature of the turning points.

(2 marks)
(total 10 marks)

Total for paper: 100 marks

End

GCE AS Level Mathematics

Statistics and Mechanics

Potential Paper 2A

Students must have Mathematical Formulae
and Statistical Tables, Calculator.

Calculator is allowed

Time allowed
1 hour 15 minutes
Total 60 marks

Write answers to 3 significant figures unless stated
otherwise

Section A: Statistics

1. There are 45 members in a sports club. 23 members play tennis, 17 members play hockey and 8 members do not play neither tennis nor hockey.

   i)   Represent the above information in a venn diagram.

            (3 marks)

   ii)   Work out the probability of picking a member who plays both tennis and hockey.

            (2 marks)

            (total 5 marks)

2. The table below provides information about the salary structure of a company.

Salary (£x)	Frequency
$200 \leq x < 300$	14
$300 \leq x < 400$	32
$400 \leq x < 600$	25
$600 \leq x < 750$	15
$750 \leq x < 900$	10
$900 \leq x < 1000$	4

   i)   Draw a histogram for the data above.

            (3 marks)

   ii)   Use linear interpolation to work out the median salary.

            (3 marks)

            (total 6 marks)

3. A random variable X has the probability function:

$$P(X = x) = \frac{4x - 3}{45}, \qquad x = 1,2,3,4,5$$

   a) Construct a table giving the probability function of x.

            (2 marks)

   b) Find $P(2.1 < x < 5.9)$

            (1 mark)

   c) Construct a table for the cumulative distribution $F(x)$.

            (2 marks)

            (total 5 marks)

4. A company produces drink cartons. The probability that any carton is damaged is 0.05.

    i)   A sample of 20 cartons is a taken. Find the probability that 3 or more cartons are damaged.

                                                                (2 marks)

            An inspector believes that the chance that a carton is damaged is different to 0.05. They take a sample of 25 cartons and 4 are damaged.

    ii)   Stating your hypothesis clearly, test the inspectors claim at the 10% significance level.

                                                                (5 marks)
                                                                (total 7 marks)

5. There are x apples in a bag. 9 of them are green and the rest are red. The probability of eating 2 red apples is 0.4.

    i)   Work out the value of x.

                                                                (5 marks)

    ii)   Hence, or otherwise, work out the probability of eating at least one red apple.

                                                                (2 marks)
                                                                (total 7 marks)

Total for this section: 30 marks

Section B: Mechanics

6. A ball is projected vertically upwards with speed $18ms^{-1}$ from a point 5m above the ground.

    i) Calculate the greatest height reached by the ball above the ground.

    (3 marks)

    ii) Calculate the speed of the ball when it hits the ground.

    (2 marks)

    iii) Calculate the time spent by the ball 12m above the ground.

    (4 marks)
    (total 9 marks)

7. A particle P moves along a straight line. At time t seconds, the velocity $v\ ms^{-1}$ of P is modelled as

    $$v = 8t - t^2 - \alpha, \ t \geq 0, \text{where } \alpha \text{ is a constant}$$

    i) Find the acceleration of P at t seconds.

    (2 marks)

    The particle P is instantaneously at rest when $t = 6$

    ii) Find the other value of t when P is instantaneously at rest.

    (4 marks)

    iii) Find the total distance travelled by P in the interval $0 \leq t \leq 3$.

    (4 marks)
    (total 10 marks)

8. A car is towing a trailer along a straight horizontal road by means of a horizontal towbar. The mass of the car is 1500 kg. The mass of the trailer is 900 kg. The car and the trailer are modelled as particles and the towbar as a light inextensible bar. The resistances to motion of the car and the trailer are assumed to be constant and of magnitude 750 N and 450 N respectively. The driving force on the car, due to its engine, is F N and the acceleration of the car is $1.5ms^{-1}$.

Find

    i)   the value of F

(3 marks)

    ii)   the magnitude of the tension in the towbar.

(3 marks)

When the car and the trailer are moving at a speed of $15ms^{-1}$, the towbar breaks. Assuming the resistances to the motion are unchanged

    iii)   Work out the distance travelled by the trailer after the towbar has broken before coming to rest.

(5 marks)
(total 11 marks)

Total for section B is 30 marks

Total for paper: 60 marks

End

Section B

GCE AS Level Mathematics

Pure Mathematics

Potential Paper 1B

Students must have Mathematical Formulae
and Statistical Tables, Calculator.

Calculator is allowed

**Time allowed
2 hours
Total 100 marks**

Write answers to 3 significant figures unless stated
otherwise

1. Work out

$$\int \left(9x^2 + 4 - \frac{4}{\sqrt{x^3}}\right) dx$$

Giving each term in its simplest form.

(5 marks)

2. $x^2 - 6x + 14 = (x - a)^2 + b$, where a and b are integers.

   i)   Find the values of a & b.

(2marks)

   ii)   Sketch the graph of $y = x^2 - 6x + 14$, clearly showing any points of intersections with coordinate axes.

(3 marks)

   iii) Find the value of the discriminant.
         Explain how the sign of the discriminant relates to your sketch in part (ii).

(2 marks)
(total 7 marks)

3. The line l_1 has equation $y = 2x + 3$ and the line l_2 has equation $6x + 2y - 5 = 0$.

   i)   Find the gradient of l_2.

(2 marks)

   The lines l_1 & l_2 intersect at the point P.

   ii)   Find the coordinates of P.

(3 marks)

   The lines l_1 & l_2 cross the line $x = 1$ at points A & B respectively.

   iii) Find the area of $\Delta\ ABP$.

(5 marks)
(total 10 marks)

4. Solve the simultaneous equations.

$$y - 5x + 3 = 0$$
$$y^2 - x - 3x^2 = 0$$

(7 marks)

5. $f(x) = (1 + ax)^5$

i)   Find the first 4 terms, in ascending powers of x, in the binomial expansion of $(1 + ax)^5$, where (a) is a non-zero constant.

(3marks)

Given that in the expansion, the coefficient of x^2 is 3 times the coefficient of x.

ii)   Find the value of a.

(3 marks)

iii)   Hence, or otherwise work out the coefficient of x^3 term.

(1 mark)
(total 7 marks)

6. Solve the following inequalities.

a) $x^2 - x - 2 < 0$

(4 marks)

b) $2x + 4 \geq 3$

(2 marks)

c) Both $x^2 - x - 2 < 0$ & $2x + 4 \geq 3$.

(2 marks)
(total 8 marks)

7. $y = 4x^3 - 5x^2 - 8x + 1.$
   i)   Find $\frac{dy}{dx}$.

(3 marks)

   ii)   Work out the coordinates of the stationary points.

(4 marks)

   iii)   Find $\frac{d^2y}{dx^2}$.

(2 marks)

   iv)   Determine the nature of the stationary points found in part (ii).

(2 marks)
(total 11 marks)

8. In the diagram below, $\overrightarrow{CA} = a$ & $\overrightarrow{CB} = b, AD:DB = 3:4.$

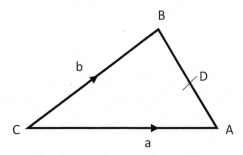

   Show that $\overrightarrow{CD} = k(a + 3b)$, where k is a constant to be found.

(4 marks)

9. The equation below has 2 real roots.

$$(k + 1)x^2 - (k + 1)x + 1 = 0$$

   Prove that
$$k \leq -1 \ or \ k \geq 3.$$

(5 marks)

10. $f(x) = 6x^3 + 23x - 6x - 8$.

    i)   Show that $(x + 4)$ is a factor of $f(x)$.

(2 marks)

    ii)   Factorise $f(x)$ fully.

(4 marks)
(total 6 marks)

11. ΔPQR is drawn below.

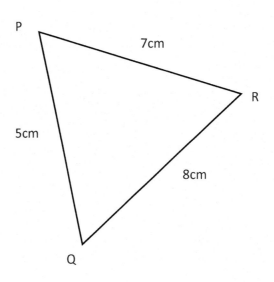

    i)   Show that $\cos P\hat{Q}R = \frac{1}{2}$.

(2 marks)

    ii)   Hence, or otherwise, Find the exact value of $\sin P\hat{Q}R$.

(3 marks)
(total 5 marks)

12. $y = x^2 - 3x$

    i)   Work out the equation of normal to the curve at point P where the
        x coordinate of P is 3.

(4 marks)

        The normal in part (i) meets the curve again at the point Q.
    ii)   Work out the coordinates of the point Q.

(3 marks)

    iii)   Calculate the area between the curve and the normal at P.

(6 marks)
(total 13 marks)

13. i) Prove that

$$\frac{1}{\sin\theta} - \sin\theta = \frac{\cos\theta}{\tan\theta}$$

(3 marks)

ii) Sketch, for $0 \le x \le 360°$, the graph of $y = \cos(x - 60)$.

(2 marks)

iii) Write down the coordinates of points where the graph in part (ii) meets the coordinate axes.

(3 marks)

iv) Solve, for $0 \le x \le 360°$, the equation

$$\cos(x - 60) = 0.85$$

Give your answers to one decimal place.

(4 marks)
(total 12 marks)

Total for paper: 100 marks

End

GCE AS Level Mathematics

Statistics and Mechanics

Potential Paper 2B

Students must have Mathematical Formulae
and Statistical Tables, Calculator.

Calculator is allowed

**Time allowed
1 hour 15 minutes
Total 60 marks**

Write answers to 3 significant figures unless stated
otherwise

Section A: Statistics

1. Marks achieved by pupils in a maths test is summarised below.

Marks	Frequency
20-50	18
50-60	10
60-80	20
80-95	9
95-100	2

A histogram was drawn to represent the data and the bar representing the marks 60-80 class has a width of 4cm & a height of 2cm.

a. Find the width and the height of the bar representing the marks 80-95 class.

(3 marks)

b. Find the width and the height of the bar representing the marks 50-60 class.

(3 marks)
(total 6 marks)

2. For the events A & B,

$$P(A) = 0.7, P(B) = 0.2$$

Given that the events A & B are independent.

i) Find $P(A \cap B)$

(2 marks)

ii) Draw a Venn diagram.

(2 marks)

iii) Find $P(A' \cap B)$

(2marks)
(total 6 marks)

3. A discrete random variable X has the probability function below.

x	0	1	2	3	4
$P(X = x)$	0.15	k	0.25	$3k$	0.2

Where, k is a positive constant.

i)   Find the value of k.

(2 marks)

ii)   Find $P(x > 2.8)$

(1 marks)

iii)   Construct a table for the cumulative distribution $F(x)$.

(2 marks)
(total 5 marks)

4. A company manufactures cars. The probability that a car is faulty within the first month is 0.05.

   a. A sample of 40 cars is taken. Find the probability that 5 or more cars are faulty.

(2 marks)

   An employee claims that the probability of manufacturing a faulty car is more than 0.05. They take a sample of 50 cars and 5 of them have faults.

   b. Stating your hypothesis clearly, test the employee's claim at 5% level of significance.

(5 marks)
(total 7 marks)

5. Sofia is measuring the weights of some books in a library and tabulated the following.

Weight (g)	Frequency
50-150	7
150-200	11
200-250	8
250-300	4
300-500	2

a. Use linear interpolation to estimate the interquartile range for the weights.

(3 marks)

b. Estimate the standard deviation.

(3 marks)
(total 6 marks)

Total for section A is 30 marks

Section B: Mechanics

6. A particle P moves with constant acceleration $(12i - 5j)ms^{-1}$.

   At time $t = 0$, P has a speed of $u\ ms^{-1}$.

   At time $t = 3$, P has velocity $(-3i + 4j)ms^{-1}$.

   Find the value of u.

   (5 marks)

7. A particle is projected vertically upwards from a point $8m$ above the ground with speed $28ms^{-1}$.

   Find

   i)   the greatest height reached by the particle.

   (3 marks)

   ii) the time for which the particle is more than $12m$ above the ground.

   (3 marks)

   iii) the time taken between the particle was projected and the time when it hits the ground.

   (3 marks)
   (total 9 marks)

8. A train starts from rest and accelerates uniformly at a constant rate until it reaches Vms^{-1} in 20 seconds. The train maintains this speed for the next 250 seconds before decelerating uniformly to rest. The magnitude of deceleration is 2.5 times the magnitude of the acceleration at the beginning of the journey.

   i.   Calculate the time taken for the journey.

   (3 marks)

   ii. Sketch a velocity-time graph for this information.

   (3 marks)

   Given that the total distance travelled during the journey was $8220m$.

   iii. Find the value of V.

   (3 marks)
   (total 9 marks)

9. Two particles A & B have masses $12kg$ & $15kg$ respectively. The particles are connected by a light inextensible string which passes over a smooth fixed pulley.

   Initially, particles A & B are $2.5m$ above the ground. The particles are released from rest with the string taught and the hanging parts of the string vertical.

   After B strikes the ground, A continues to move vertically upwards freely under gravity but does not reach the pulley.

   Calculate the greatest height reached by the particle A above the ground.

   (7 marks)

   Total for section B is 30 marks

   Total for paper: 60 marks

   End

Section C

GCE AS Level Mathematics

Pure Mathematics

Potential Paper 1C

Students must have Mathematical Formulae
and Statistical Tables, Calculator.

Calculator is allowed

Time allowed
2 hours
Total 100 marks

Write answers to 3 significant figures unless stated
otherwise

GCE AS Level Mathematics Potential Exam Papers

1. Prove algebraically that the difference between two odd integers is always even.

(4 marks)

2. Find

$$\int \frac{3}{4}x^2 - 3\sqrt{x} + 2)dx$$

Giving your answer in its simplest form.

(4 marks)

3. $\overrightarrow{BA} = 2a, \overrightarrow{BC} = 3c, BCD$ & PQD are straight lines, P is midpoint of AB & $AQ:QC = 2:1$.

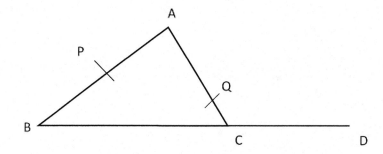

Work out $\overrightarrow{CD}$

(6 marks)

4. $A(-1,4)$, $B(3,3)$. AB meets y-axis at P.

Work out perpendicular to AB at P.

(6 marks)

5. $\log_3(x^2 - 1) + \log_3(2x + 5) = 3$

Find x.

(5 marks)

6. $y = 16 + 6x - x^2$
i) Show that $y = a - (x - b)^2$ where a and are integers to be found.

(3 marks)

ii) Hence, find maximum point of y.

(2 marks)
(total 5 marks)

7.

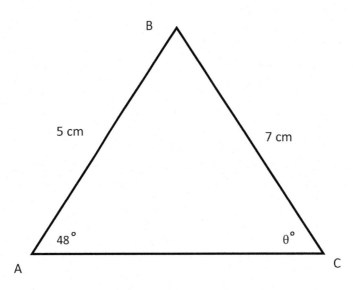

i) Find possible values of θ.

(4 marks)

Given that θ is the smaller value.
ii) Find the value of AC.

(2 marks)
(total 6 marks)

8. An open top cylinder has volume $108\pi cm^3$.

i) Show that the surface area (A) is

$$A = \pi r^2 + \frac{216\pi}{r}$$

(4 marks)

ii) Work out the minimum surface area of the cylinder.

(4 marks)

iii) Justify the area found in part ii) is a minimum.

(2marks)
(total 10 marks)

9. $f(x) = x^3 - 19x - 30$

i) Factorise $f(x)$ fully.

(5 marks)

ii) Hence, sketch the graph of $y = f(x)$, clearly stating all points of intersection with coordinate axes.

(4 marks)
(total 9 marks)

10. Prove from first principles that derivative of e^x is e^x.

(5 marks)

11. i) Work out the first 3 terms of the expansion, $\left(2 - \dfrac{x}{b}\right)^8$ in terms of b where $b > 0$ *and b is an interger.*

(3 marks)

ii) Given that the 3rd term of the expansion is 112.

Find the value of b.

(3 marks)

iii) Hence, find the coefficient of the fourth term.

(2 mark)
(8 marks)

12. i) Show that $7 - 8\cos\theta - 4\sin^2\theta = 0$, can be written as

$$4\cos^2\theta - 8\cos\theta + 3 = 0$$

(3 marks)

ii) Hence, solve for $-60° \leq \theta \leq 180$

$$7 - 8\cos 3x - 4\sin^2 3x = 0$$

Giving your answers to 1 decimal place, where appropriate.

(4 marks)
(total 7 marks)

13. $f(x) = e^{3x-2} - 1$

a) State the range of f

(1 mark)

b) The curve $y = f(x)$ meets the $y - axis$ at P & $x - axis$ at Q.
Work out exact coordinates of points P & Q.

(4 marks)

c) Find the equation of the normal to the curve at P.

(5 marks)
(total 10 marks)

14. The circle C has equation,

$$x^2 + y^2 - 2x + 4y = 30$$

i) Find

a) the coordinates of the centre of circle C.

(1 mark)

b) the radius of the circle C.

(2 marks)

ii) The line with equation $y = mx$, where m is a constant is a diameter of the circle.

Work out the value m.

(4 marks)
(total 7 marks)

15. A parabola has equation $y = x^2 - 2x + 3$

i) The curve has a minimum point at P.

Work out the coordinates of P.

(2 marks)

ii) The normal to curve at $x = 2$ meets the $x - axis$ at Q.

Calculate the area bounded by the curve, the normal at $x = 2$ & the coordinate axes.

(6 marks)
(total 8 marks)

Total for paper: 100 marks

End

GCE AS Level Mathematics

Statistics and Mechanics

Potential Paper 2C

Students must have Mathematical Formulae
and Statistical Tables, Calculator.

Calculator is allowed

Time allowed
1 hour 15 minutes
Total 60 marks

Write answers to 3 significant figures unless stated
otherwise

Section A: Statistics

1. Table below shows marks achieved by a class of mathematics students in a school.

Marks	Frequency
21-50	9
51-70	10
71-80	7
81-100	6

i) Represent above information in a histogram.

(3 marks)

ii) Estimate the probability of a student achieving less than 60 marks.

(3 marks)
(total 6 marks)

2. Below is a list of heights of 10 students in centimetres.

172, 165, 171, 161, 167, 155, 180, 166, 176, 163

i) Calculate the median height and the interquartile range.

(4 marks)

ii) Determine if there are any outliers.

(2 marks)

iii) Draw a box plot.

(2 marks)
(total 8 marks)

3. For the events P & Q.

$$P(P) = 0.7, P(Q) = 0.4 \ \& \ P(P \cup Q)' = 0.18$$

a) Find $P(P \cap Q)$

(2 marks)

b) Draw a Venn diagram

(2 marks)

c) Determine, whether P & Q are independent.

(2 marks)
(total 6 marks)

4. The manager of a company wants to find out what his customers think about company's closing times and decides to carry out a survey.

i) Suggest a suitable sampling frame for the survey.

(1 mark)

ii) Identify the sampling units.

(1 mark)

The manager decides to ask 15 customers towards the end of a day.

iii) State the sampling technique used.

(1 mark)

iv) Give one disadvantage of this technique.

(1 mark)
(total 4 marks)

5. Jim has a 25% chance of losing a game.

a) Calculate the probability of losing at least 6 times if he plays 50 games.

(2 marks)

In the 20 games he has played, he lost only 3 times.

b) Test at 5% level of significance whether Jim's chance of losing has decreased. Clearly state your hypothesis.

(4 marks)
(total 6 marks)

Total for section A is 30 marks

Section B: Mechanics

6. A ball is dropped from a point 75m above the ground.

Calculate

i) the time it takes for the ball to reach the ground.

(3 marks)

ii) the speed at which the ball hits the ground with.

(3 marks)
(total 6 marks)

7. The resultant of two forces F_1 & F_2 is parallel to the vector $2i + 3j$.

Given that $F_1 = 4i - 3j$ & $F_2 = ki + 3kj$.
Where k is a positive constant.

Find the value of k.

(5 marks)

8. A train starts from rest and accelerates uniformly until it reaches a velocity of $V\ ms^{-1}$ in 30 seconds. The train then maintains this velocity for 6 minutes before decelerating in 1.2 times the magnitude of the acceleration at the beginning of the journey.

i) Work out the total time taken for the journey.

(3 marks)

ii) Sketch a velocity-time graph.

(3 marks)

Given that the total distance travelled was 16.275km.

iii) Find the value V.

(3 marks)
(total 9 marks)

9. Diagram below shows particles A & B of masses $3kg$ & $5kg$ respectively connected by a light inextensible string which passes a smooth pulley attached to the end of a table. Particle A experiences a frictional force of 14N & particle B hangs vertically down $1.8m$ above ground as shown.

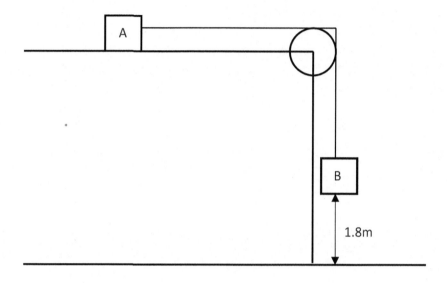

a) Find acceleration of the system and tension in the string.

(5 marks)

b) Work out, the time taken by B to reach the ground.

(5 marks)
(total 10 marks)

Total for section B is 30 marks

Total for paper: 60 marks

End

Section D

GCE AS Level Mathematics

Pure Mathematics

Potential Paper 1D

Students must have Mathematical Formulae
and Statistical Tables, Calculator.

Calculator is allowed

**Time allowed
2 hours
Total 100 marks**

Write answers to 3 significant figures unless stated
otherwise

1. Points A & B are such that A (5, 1), B (7, -3).

   i)   Find midpoint of AB.

(1 mark)

   ii)   Find equation of perpendicular line to AB through its midpoint.

(4 marks)
(total 5 marks)

2. The curve C has equation $y = 3x^2 - 5x - 1$

   i)   Find gradient of C at $x = 2$

(3 marks)

   ii)   Hence or otherwise, work out equation of tangent to curve at $x = 2$

(3 marks)
(total 6 marks)

3. Vectors A & B are such that

$$A = 4i - 5j, \qquad B = 8i + 3j$$

   i)   Work out $\overrightarrow{BA}$

(2 marks)

   ii)   Find $|\overrightarrow{BA}|$, giving your answer in simplified surd form.

(2 marks)
(total 4 marks)

4. $f(x) = 2x^3 + 3x^2 - 32x + 15$

     i)   Use factor theorem to show that $(x + 5)$ is a factor of $f(x)$.

(2 marks)

     ii)   Hence, factorise $f(x)$ fully.

(3 marks)

(total 5 marks)

5. Given that $f(x) = 3x^3 - 4x^2 + \dfrac{4}{x^2} + \dfrac{2}{x^3}$

     i)   Find $f'(x)$

(3 marks)

     ii)   Find $\int f(x)dx$

(4 marks)

(total 7 marks)

6. Prove from first principles, that the derivative of x^3 is $3x^2$.

(4 marks)

7. a) Expand $(3 - 2x)^9$ up to and including x^3 term.

(4 marks)

b) Using your answer to part (a), work out $(2.98)^9$ to 4 decimal places.

(4 marks)

(total 8 marks)

8. Calculate the area of triangle ABC.

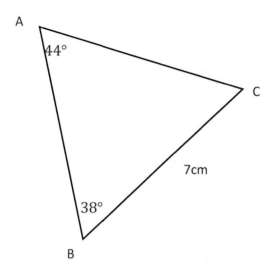

(4 marks)

9. Solve the following equation and write your answers to 1 decimal place.

$$6 \sin^2 x - \sin x - 1 = 0 \; for \; 0 \leq x \leq 360°$$

(5 marks)

10. The equation
$$px^2 + 3px - 2 = 0, where \; p \; is \; a \; constant$$

has real roots. Find possible values of p.

(4 marks)

11. Show that $(3n + 1)^2 - (3n - 1)^2$ is a multiple of 12 for all values of n. Where n is an integer.

(4 marks)

12. Solve for x.

$$(3^{2x+2}) - 5(3^{x+1}) + 4 = 0$$

(6 marks)

13. $f(x) = x^3 - 8x^2 + 16x$

    i)   Factorise $f(x)$ completely

(2 marks)

    ii)   Sketch the graph of $y = f(x)$

(2 marks)

The point $(2, 0)$ lies on the curve with equation

$y = (x - k)^3 - 8(x - k)^2 + 16(x - k)$, where k is a constant.

    iii)   Find possible values of k.

(4 marks)
(total 8 marks)

14. Solve the following equations

    i) $e^{2x} - 3e^x - 4 = 0$

(4 marks)

    ii) $\ln(x - 1) - \ln(2) = 3$

(3 marks)
(total 7 marks)

15. The curves C_1 & C_2 are $y = e^x$ & $y = -x^2$ respectively.

Point P lies on C_2 such that x-coordinate of P is -3.

  i)   Work out y-coordinate of P.

(1 mark)

  ii)   Work out tangent to C_2 at P.

(2 marks)

Above tangent meets y-axis at Q.

  iii) Work out the area bounded by the line PQ, the curve C_2 & y-axis.

(6 marks)
(total 9 marks)

16. AB is a diameter of a circle centred C where $A(2, -3)$ & $B(8, 1)$

  i)   Work out the coordinates of point C

(2 marks)

  ii)   Work out the radius of circle

(2 marks)

  iii) Hence, write down the equation of above circle.

(1 mark)
(total 5 marks)

17. An open top fish tank is to be designed in the shape of a cuboid using glass. The volume of the tank needs to be 8000 cm^3. The width and the height of the tank are x cm each and the length is y cm.

 i)   Show that surface area (A) of glass required is

$$A = 2x^2 + \frac{24000}{x}$$

(4 marks)

 $10cm^2$ of glass costs £1.

 ii)   Work out the minimum possible cost of the tank?

(5 marks)
(total 9 marks)

Total for paper: 100 marks

End

GCE AS Level Mathematics

Statistics and Mechanics

Potential Paper 2D

Students must have Mathematical Formulae
and Statistical Tables, Calculator.

Calculator is allowed

**Time allowed
1 hour 15 minutes
Total 60 marks**

Write answers to 3 significant figures unless stated
otherwise

GCE AS Level Mathematics Potential Exam Papers

Section A: Statistics

1. x is the number of people visiting a surgery each day over n days.

   $n = 12, \sum x = 111, \sum x^2 = 1395$

   i)   Calculate mean number of people per day.

                                                                    (2 marks)

   ii)   Calculate the standard deviation.

                                                                    (2 marks)
                                                            (total 4 marks)

2. The heights of some students are given below.

Heights(cm)	Frequency	
120-149	7	
150-159	6	
160-179	8	
180-199	5	
200-209	1	

   i)   Represent above data on a histogram.

                                                                    (3 marks)

   ii)   Work out interquartile range

                                                                    (4 marks)

   iii)   Calculate the percentage of students between 162cm and 176cm.

                                                                    (4 marks)
                                                            (total 11 marks)

3. There are 30 people in a group and 16 of them like chicken and 20 like eggs. 2 of the them do not like both.

   i)   Work out probability of a randomly selected person liking both.

   (3 marks)

   ii)   Draw a Venn diagram.

   (2 marks)
   (total 5 marks)

4. Past records show that 20% of patients did not recover from an illness in a hospital after a treatment.

   A new treatment was introduced and a sample of 30 patients who had the illness were treated using the new treatment. Doctors believe that the new treatment has a different recovery chance to the previous one.

   i)   Write down the hypotheses that should be used to test the doctors claim.

   (1 mark)

   ii)   Using a 5% level of significance, find critical regions for a two-tailed test to answer doctors' belief. (each tail must be lesson than 2.5%)

   (3 marks)

   iii)   Work out the actual significance level of a test based on your critical regions in part (ii).

   (1 mark)

   Out of the 30 patients in the sample above only 4 patients did not recover using the new treatment.

   iv)   Comment on the doctors' belief.

   (1 mark)
   (total 6 marks)

5. A veterinarian measured the heights and ages of 10 dogs. The data is shown below.

Height(cm)	57	16	38	41	24	76	21	33	13	27
Age(years)	6	2	4	3	4	5	4	8	1	2

i. Draw a scatter graph for the information.

(2 marks)

ii. Give an interpretation of the correlation between the height and ages of the dogs.

(2 marks)
(total 4 marks)

Total for section A is 30 marks
Section B: Mechanics

6. A block of mass 10kg is moving with an acceleration of $1.7ms^{-2}$ as shown below. There is a resistance force of 15N.

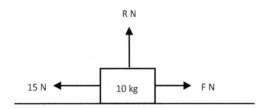

i. Work out R

(2 marks)

ii. Work out F

(3 marks)
(total 5 marks)

7. A train travels along a straight horizontal track with constant acceleration from A to C. The distance AC is x m.

   Train passes A with speed $3ms^{-1}$ and C with speed 18 ms^{-1}. Point B is such that AB is 300 m and the train takes 20 seconds to reach B from A.

   i)   Work out the speed at B.

   (4 marks)

   ii)   Find the value of x.

   (3 marks)

   iii)   Work out the time taken from C to B.

   (3 marks)
   (total 10 marks)

8. Atone is projected vertically upwards from a height of x m from the ground with a speed of $18ms^{-1}$. The stone hits the ground 6 seconds later.

   i)   Find the value x.

   (3 marks)

   ii)   Work out the greatest height reached by the stone.

   (3 marks)
   (total 6 marks)

9. Two particles A & B of masses 5kg & 3kg respectively are connected by a light inextensible string which passes over a smooth pulley as shown below.

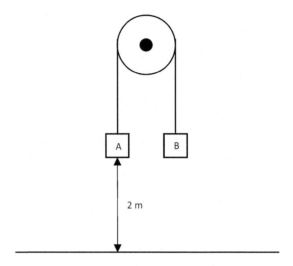

Particles are 2m above ground. The system is released from rest with the string taut. When A strikes the ground, B still has not reached the pulley.

i)   Work out the initial acceleration of the system.

(3 marks)

ii)   Hence, work out the tension in the string before B hits the ground.

(2 marks)

iii)   Work out the greatest height reached by B.

(4 marks)
(total 9 marks)

Total for section B is 30 marks

Total for paper: 60 marks

End

Section E

GCE AS Level Mathematics

Pure Mathematics

Potential Paper 1E

Students must have Mathematical Formulae
and Statistical Tables, Calculator.

Calculator is allowed

Time allowed
2 hours
Total 100 marks

Write answers to 3 significant figures unless stated
otherwise

1. Find the first 3 terms in ascending powers of x of the binomial expansion of

$$(2 - x)^5$$

   and simplify each term.

   (4 marks)

2. $6\cos^2 \theta + sin\theta - 5 = 0$

   i)   Show that above equation can be written as

   $$6 \sin^2 \theta - sin\theta - 1 = 0$$

   (2 marks)

   ii)   Solve for $0 \le \theta \le 360$

   $$6 \sin^2 \theta - sin\theta - 1 = 0$$

   (4 marks)
   (total 6 marks)

3. Two points A & B are $(1, -4)$ & $(3, \ 8)$ respectively.

   i)   Work out the mid-point of AB.

   (2 marks)

   ii)   Work out the equation of the perpendicular line to AB through its mid-point.

   (4 marks)
   (total 6 marks)

4. Points P & Q are $P(2, -5)$ & $Q(8, 11)$

     i)   Work out the vector $\overrightarrow{PQ}$.

(2 marks)

     ii)   Work out $\left|\frac{1}{2}\overrightarrow{PQ}\right|$ in simplified surd form.

(3 marks)

(total 5 marks)

5. $f(x) = x^3 + 5x^2 - 8x + 1$

     Find the values of x for which f is increasing?

(4 marks)

6. Solve the following inequality

$$3x^2 - x - 10 < 0$$

(4 marks)

7. Work out the following integral

$$\int \left(4x^3 + \frac{1}{4x^3}\right) dx$$

(4 marks)

8. Given that the equation

$$5x^2 - px + p - 2 = 0$$

Where p is a real constant, has real roots.

i)   Show that
$$p^2 - 20p + 40 \geq 0$$

(3 marks)

ii)   Find the set of possible values of p.

(4 marks)

iii)   State the smallest value of p for which the roots are equal and hence solve the equation when p takes this value.

(3 marks)
(total 10 marks)

9. A curve has equation
$$y = x^3 - 4x^2 + 7x$$

i)   Show that the curve crosses the x-axis at only one point.

(4 marks)

The point $P(2, 6)$ lies on the curve.

ii)   Find the equation of normal to curve at P.

(4 marks)

The normal at P cuts the coordinate axes at Q & R.

iii)   Work out the distance QR.

(4 marks)
(total 12 marks)

10. The table below shows a company's growth in revenue over the years.

Year	2005	2006	2007	2008	2009
Revenue (£1000's)	58.1	67.5	80.1	105.6	138.6

The data can be represented by an exponential model of growth. Using R as annual revenue in £1000's and t as the number of years after 2000, a suitable model is

$$R = a(10^{kt})$$
where a & k are constants

i) Derive an equation for $\log_{10} R$ in terms of a, k & t.

(2 marks)

ii) Draw the graph of $\log_{10} R$ against t, drawing a best fit line.

(3 marks)

iii) Using your line, find R in terms of t.

(4 marks)

iv) According to the model, what was the revenue in year 2000?

(1 mark)

v) According to the model, when will the revenue reach £250,000?

(2 marks)
(total 12 marks)

11. $y = x^3 - 2x^2 + 5x - 1$

    i)   Find equation of tangent to curve at $x = 2$.

                                  (5 marks)

    ii)   Above tangents meets x=axis at A & y-axis at B. Work out coordinates of A & B.

                                  (4 marks)

    iii)   Work out the area of triangle AOB where O is the origin.

                                  (3 marks)
                             (total 12 marks)

12. Work out the area between the curve $y = x^2 - 6x + 11$ & the line $y = 6$.

                                  (6 marks)

13. $A(1, -4)$ & $B(7, 6)$. Where AB is a diameter of a circle centred at C.

    i)   Work out the coordinates if centre and radius of the circle.

                                  (4 marks)

    ii)   Work out the equation of the tangent to circle at A in the form $ax + by + c = 0$ where a, b, c are integers.

                                  (5 marks)

    iii)   Above tangent meets x-axis at P & y-axis at Q. Work out the area of triangle OPQ, where O is the origin.

                                  (6 marks)
                             (total 15 marks)

Total for paper: 100 marks

End

GCE AS Level Mathematics

Statistics and Mechanics

Potential Paper 2E

Students must have Mathematical Formulae
and Statistical Tables, Calculator.

Calculator is allowed

Time allowed
1 hour 15 minutes
Total 60 marks

Write answers to 3 significant figures unless stated
otherwise

Section A: Statistics

1. John asked 40 people which sandwich they prefer out of Cheese, Ham & Egg.

   2 people like all three
   6 like cheese and ham
   3 like cheese and egg
   5 like egg and ham
   13 like cheese
   17 like ham
   11 like egg

   i)   Complete a Venn diagram above information

   (3 marks)

   ii)   Work out the probability of a person liking exactly 2 types of sandwiches only.

   (2 marks)
   (total 5 marks)

2. The discrete random variable $X \sim B(30, 0.45)$

   a) Work out $P(7 \leq x < 11)$

   (2 marks)

   Previous records show that a player loses 20% of his matches. In a random sample of 20 matches, he lost 9 matches.

   b) Test at the 10% level of significance whether the percentage of this players loses have increased clearly stating your hypothesis.

   (5 marks)
   (total 7 marks)

3. Scores of cricket innings are listed below.

151	234	451	199	201	302	195	276

i)   Work out the mean score

(1 mark)

ii)   Calculate the standard deviation

(3 marks)

iii)   Find median & Interquartile range

(4 marks)
(total 8 marks)

4. Two events C & D are independent.

$$P(C) = 0.6 \ \& \ P(D) = 0.5$$

i)   Find $P(C \cap D)$

(2 marks)

ii)   Represent all probabilities on a Venn diagram

(2 marks)

iii)   Find $P(C' \cup D)$

(3 marks)

iv)   Find $P(C \cap D')$

(3 marks)
(total 10 marks)

Total for section A is 30 marks

Section B: Mechanics

5. A particle Q of mass 0.7kg moves with the action of a force $F\ N$. The acceleration of Q is $(3i - 4j)ms^{-2}$.

    a. Find the angle between the acceleration and vector j

    (3 marks)

    b. Work out the magnitude of F

    (3 marks)
    (total 6 marks)

6. A ball is projected vertically upwards with speed $16ms^{-1}$ from a point $4m$ above ground.

    i)   What is the maximum height reached by the ball?

    (3 marks)

    ii)   What is the time of flight?

    (3 marks)

    iii) Calculate the difference when the ball is $7m$ above the ground level.

    (4 marks)
    (total 10 marks)

7. A train passes a point A with speed $8 ms^{-1}$. It accelerates at a constant rate and 10 seconds later the train is passing point B with speed $18\ ms^{-1}$.

   Work out

   i)   the acceleration of the train?

   (3 marks)

   ii)   distance AB

   (3 marks)

   iii)   the time taken to travel 75% of the distance AB.

   (3 marks)
   (total 9 marks)

8. A particle moving in a straight line through a point O has displacement $x\ m$, where
$$x = 2t^3 - 20t^2 - 14t$$

   i.   initial velocity of the particle.

   (2 marks)

   ii.   When the acceleration is zero.

   (3 marks)
   (total 5 marks)

Total for section B is 30 marks

Total for paper: 60 marks

End

Section F

GCE AS Level Mathematics

Pure Mathematics

Potential Paper 1F

Students must have Mathematical Formulae
and Statistical Tables, Calculator.

Calculator is allowed

**Time allowed
2 hours
Total 100 marks**

Write answers to 3 significant figures unless stated
otherwise

1. AB is a diameter of a circle with centre C. Where $A(4, 9)$ & $B(8, 11)$

    i.   Work out the centre and radius of the circle.

(4 marks)

    ii.   Write down the equation of circle.

(1 mark)
(total 5 marks)

2. Find $\frac{dy}{dx}$ of the following

    i. $y = 4x^3 - 10x^2 + 7x - 3$

(2 marks)

    ii. $y = \frac{1}{x} - \frac{1}{x^2}$

(3 marks)

    iii. $y = (x + 3)(2x - \frac{1}{x})$

(4 marks)
(total 9 marks)

3. Rationalise the following

   i) $\dfrac{2}{1-\sqrt{2}}$

(2 marks)

   ii) $\dfrac{3+\sqrt{7}}{3-\sqrt{7}}$

(3 marks)

   iii) $\dfrac{4+2\sqrt{3}}{6-3\sqrt{3}}$

(4 marks)
(total 9marks)

4. Solve the following inequalities

   i) $5x - 3 \leq 7 + 6x$

(2 marks)

   ii) $-3 \leq \dfrac{3x-1}{2} < 5$

(3 marks)

   iii) $2x^2 - 5x - 12 > 0$

(4 marks)
(total 9 marks)

5.
   i.   Expand $(2 - x)^3$ fully.

(3 marks)

   ii.   Hence or otherwise, expand $(2 - y - y^2)^3$

(5 marks)
(total 8 marks)

6. $P(4,7), \ Q(9,-1)$

Work out equation of perpendicular line to PQ through its midpoint. Write your answer in the form

$$ax + by + c = 0, where\ a, b\ \&\ c\ are\ integers.$$

(6 marks)

7. Work out following integrals

   i) $\int_1^3 (12x^2 - 6x + 1)dx$

(3 marks)

   ii) $\int_{-1}^0 (3x - 2)^2 dx$

(3 marks)

   iii) $\int_2^3 (2x - 1)(3x + 5)dx$

(4 marks)
(total 10marks)

8. $x^2 - 2px + 2p + 3 = 0$ has two distinct real roots. Work out possible values of p.

(6 marks)

9. $f(x) = 2x^3 - 5x^2 - 14x + 8$

    (i)   Factorise $f(x)$ fully.

(4 marks)

    (ii)   Hence solve, $f(x) = 0$.

(3 marks)

    (iii)   Sketch $y = f(x)$.

(3 marks)
(total 10 marks)

10. An open top glass fish tank has length ycm and width & height both are xcm each. The volume of the tank is $2400cm^3$.

    i)   Show that surface area (A) of the tank is

$$A = 2x^2 + \frac{7200}{x}$$

(4 marks)

    ii)   Work out the minimum possible surface area of the tank.

(3 marks)

    iii)   Confirm that the area you have found in part (ii) is a minimum.

(3 marks)

Cost of glass is 12 pence per $10cm^2$.

    iv)   Work out the minimum cost of the tank.

(2 marks)
(total 12 marks)

11. Solve the following for x.

$$2^{2x+2} - 11(2^x) + 6 = 0$$

(5 marks)

12. $y = 2x^3 - 21x^2 + 72x - 3$

    i)   Work out the coordinates of turning points of above curve.

(6 marks)

          The curve cuts the y-axis at P.

    ii)   Find the equation of normal to curve at point P.

(5 marks)
(total 11 marks)

Total for paper: 100 marks

End

GCE AS Level Mathematics

Statistics and Mechanics

Potential Paper 2F

Students must have Mathematical Formulae
and Statistical Tables, Calculator.

Calculator is allowed

Time allowed
1 hour 15 minutes
Total 60 marks

Write answers to 3 significant figures unless stated
otherwise

Section A: Statistics

1. A random variable X is defined by $X \sim B(25, 0.35)$

   a. Work out the following

      i) $P(x = 10)$

(2 marks)

      ii) $P(x > 10)$

(2 marks)

      iii) $P(3 \leq x < 9)$

(3 marks)

   b. State two conditions under which a random variable can be modelled by a binomial distribution.

(2 marks)

(total 9 marks)

2. Details of daily mileage by some drivers are given below.

Miles Driven	Number of Drivers		
0-19	15		
20-39	19		
40-49	16		
50-89	8		
90-100	5		

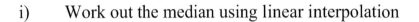

i) Work out the median using linear interpolation

(3 marks)

ii) Work out interquartile range

(4 marks)

iii) Calculate $P_{60} - P_{45}$

(4 marks)

iv) Find standard deviation

(3 marks)
(total 14 marks)

3. The probability of Jerry hitting a target first time is 0.6. If he hit the target first time the probability of him hitting the target in his second go is 0.85. If he had missed the target first time the probability of him hitting the target second time 0.5.

    i)   Draw a tree diagram to show all possibilities.

                                                           (2 marks)

    ii)   Work out the probability of hitting the target at least once.

                                                           (2 marks)

    iii)   Given that jerry has hit the target, work out the probability that he has hit the target with his second attempt.

                                                          (3 marks)
                                                (total 7 marks)

Total for section A is 30 marks

Section B: Mechanics

4. A particle A of mass 3kg is resting on a smooth horizontal table and is attached to a light inextensible string which passes over smooth fixed pulley. On the other side of the pulley particle B of mass 2kg hangs vertically below the pulley 1.6m above the ground as shown below.

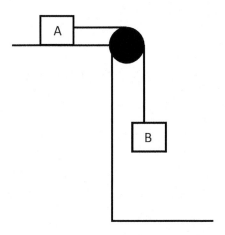

The system is released from rest with the string taut. The particle A does not reach the pulley before B hits the ground.

i)   Calculate the tension in the string before B hits the ground.

(4 marks)

ii)   Find the time taken by B to reach the ground.

(5 marks)
(total 9 marks)

5. A particle A moves in a straight line so that at time t seconds, its velocity is v ms^{-1} given by

$$v = \begin{cases} 4t - t^2, & 0 \leq t < 2 \\ 8 - 2t, & t \geq 2 \end{cases}$$

a. Work out acceleration of A when $t = 1$

(3 marks)

b. Find the total distance travelled by A during the first 5 seconds.

(7 marks)

(total 10 marks)

6. A stone is projected vertically upwards with speed $15ms^{-1}$ from a point $12m$ above sea level.

i)   Work out the maximum height reached by the stone above sea level.

(3 marks)

ii)   Calculate the total time taken to reach the sea level.

(2 marks)

iii)   Work out the time period for which the stone is $15m$ above sea level.

(3 marks)

(total 8 marks)

7. A particle P of mass 1.5kg moves under the actions of a force F N. The acceleration of P is $(4i - 5j)ms^{-2}$.

Calculate the magnitude of force F?

(3 marks)

Total for section B is 30 marks

Total for paper: 60 marks

End

Answers

Paper A1	Paper A2
1. a) $6561 + 17,496kx + 20,412k^2x^2 + 13,608k^3x^3$ b) $k = 5$	1. i) correctly draw venn diagram ii) $\frac{1}{15}$
2. i) $a = -14$, ii) $x = 1$	2. i) correctly drawn histogram ii) £396.88
3. i) $a - 5$ & $b - -15$, ii) $(x - 3)(2x + 1)(x + 5)$ iii) sketch through $(0, -15), (-5, 0), \left(-\frac{1}{2}, 0\right)$ & $(3, 0)$	3. i) correct table ii) $\frac{29}{45}$, iii) correct table
4. $\frac{1}{12}x^4 + \frac{1}{2}x^{-1} + c$	4. i) 0.0755, ii) $0.0341 < 0.05$ reject H_0, inspector is correct.
5. a) Prove vector PO is parallel to vector OQ. b) $\sqrt{13}ms^{-1}$	5. i) $x = 0.25$, ii) 0.6
6. i) a sketch with points $\left(-\frac{5}{8}, -\frac{41}{16}\right)$ & $(0, -1)$ ii) 13, iii) $13 + 4h$, iv) as $h \to 0, f'(x) \to 13$	6. i) 21.5m, ii) $7\sqrt{2}ms^{-1}$, iii) 2.8s
7. i) $x \geq -\frac{5}{2}$, ii) $x < -1$ & $x > 3$, iii) $-\frac{5}{2} \leq x < -1$ & $x > 3$	7. i) $8 - 2t$, ii) 2s. iii) $\frac{91}{3}m$
8. 69.82cm	8. a)4800N, b)1800N, c)225m
9. i) $\alpha = 0.25$, & $\beta = 2500$, ii) 8.61 years	
10. Let $n = 2m$ for any integer m and consider both odd and even cases.	
11. i) $80°, 100°, 200°, 220°$, ii) $30°, 41.8°, 138.2°, 150°$	
12. i) $(x - 6)^2 + (y - 10)^2 = \frac{196}{5}$ ii) $20 \ or - 6$	
13. i) 2.18, ii) $-\frac{1}{3}$	
14. a) $\frac{dy}{dx} = 3x^2 - 10x - 8$ b)$(-\frac{2}{3}, \frac{184}{27})$ & $(4, -44)$ c)$\frac{d^2y}{dx^2} = 6x - 10$ d)$\left(-\frac{2}{3}, \frac{184}{27}\right)$ max & $(4, -44)$ min	

Paper B1	Paper B2
15. $3x^3 + 4x + 8x^{-\frac{1}{2}} + c$	9. a) width $3cm$ & height $1.2cm$ b) width $2cm$ & height $2cm$.
16. i) $a = 3, b = 5$, ii) correct sketch, iii) $b^2 - 4ac = -20$, no intersections with x axis.	10. i) 0.14, ii) correct Venn diagram, iii) 0.06
17. i) -3, ii) $P(-\frac{1}{10}, \frac{14}{5})$, iii) $\frac{121}{40} units^2$	11. i) $k = 0.1$, ii) 0.5, iii)

For Paper B2, question 11 iii) table:

x	0	1	2	3	4
$F(x)$	0.15	0.25	0.5	0.8	1

Paper B1	Paper B2
18. when $x = 1, y = 2$ and when $x = \frac{9}{22}, y = -\frac{21}{22}$.	12. a) 0.0480 b) $P(X \geq 5) = 0.1036 > 0.05$ Insufficient evidence to reject H_0. Employee's claim is wrong.
19. i) $1 + 5ax + 10a^2x^2 + 10a^{3x^3} + \cdots$ ii) $a = \frac{3}{2}$, iii) $\frac{135}{4}$	13. a) $75\ marks$, b) $75.9\ marks$.
20. i) $-1 < x < 2$ with a sketch. ii) $x \geq -\frac{1}{2}$ iii) $-\frac{1}{2} \leq x < 2$ with evidence.	14. $43.4ms^{-1}$
21. i) $\frac{dy}{dx} = 12x^2 - 10x - 8$, ii) $\left(\frac{4}{3}, -\frac{245}{27}\right)$ & $\left(-\frac{1}{2}, \frac{13}{4}\right)$ iii) $\frac{d^2y}{dx^2} = 24x - 10$ iv) $\left(\frac{4}{3}, -\frac{245}{27}\right)$ is a minimum & $\left(-\frac{1}{2}, \frac{13}{4}\right)$ is a maximum.	15. i) $48m$, ii) $5.42s$, iii) $5.99s$ 16. i) $278s$, ii) correct sketch, iii) $31.1ms^{-1}$ 17. $5.28m$
22. $k = \frac{1}{7}$	
23. Correct proof.	
24. i) $f(-4) = 0$, ii) $(x + 4)(2x - 1)(3x + 1)$	
25. i) proof using cosine rule, ii) $\frac{\sqrt{3}}{2}$	
26. i) $3y + x - 3 = 0$, ii) $Q\left(-\frac{1}{3}, \frac{10}{9}\right)$, iii) $\frac{500}{81} units^2$	
27. i) correct proof, ii) corrrect sketch iii) $\left(0, \frac{1}{2}\right), (150,0), (330,0)$ iv) $x = 28.2°, 91.8°$	

Paper C1	Paper C2
1. proof	1. i) histogram drawn
	ii) $\frac{7}{16}$
2. $\frac{1}{4}x^3 - 2x^{\frac{3}{2}} + 2x + c$	
	2. i) median = 166.5cm & IQR = 10.5cm
3. $\overrightarrow{CD} = 3c$	ii) No outliers
	iii)Box plot shown
4. $4y - 16x - 15 = 0$	
	3. a)$P(P \cap Q) = 0.28$
5. $x = 2, \frac{-18+\sqrt{209}}{2}$	b) Venn diagram
	c) P & Q are independent
6. i. $a = 25, b = 3,$	
ii. (3,25)	4. i) customers in the shop towards closing time
	ii) customers
7. i) 32.1°, 147.9°,	iii) Non random & can be biased
ii) 2.25cm	
	5. a) 0.9930
8. i) proof,	b) no evidence to reject H_0, number of losses have
ii) $213.7cm^2$,	not decreased.
iii) show $\frac{d^2y}{dx^2} > 0$	
	6. i) t = 3.91 s
9. i) $(x + 2)(x - 5)(x + 3)$,	ii) $38.3ms^{-1}$
ii) sketch	
	7. k = 6
10. proof	
	8. i) 6 minutes and 55 seconds
11. i)$256 - \frac{1024x}{b} + \frac{1792x^2}{b^2} + \cdots$,	ii) sketch
ii)$b = 4$,	iii) $42ms^{-1}$
iii) $-35x^3$	
	9. a) $a = 4.38ms^{-2}$ & $T = 27.14 N$
12. $x = -20°, 20°, 100°, 140°$	b) $t = 0.91s$
13. a) $f(x) > -1$,	
b) $P(0, e^{-2} - 1), Q(\frac{2}{3}, 0)$	
c) $y + 1 - \frac{3}{e^2} = -\frac{e^2}{3}x$	
14. i) a) $(1, -2)$, b) $r = \sqrt{35}$	
ii) $m = -2$	
15. i) $P(1,2)$	
ii) $\frac{41}{3} units^2$	

Paper D1	**Paper D2**
1. i) $(6, -1)$ ii) $y - 2x + 13 = 0$	1. i) 9.25 ii) 5.54
2. i) $\frac{dy}{dx} = 7$ ii) $y - 7x + 13 = 0$	2. i) histogram ii) 30 iii) 20.7%
3. i) $\binom{-4}{-8}$ ii) $4\sqrt{5}$	3. i) $\frac{4}{15}$ ii) Venn diagram
4. i) proof ii) $(x + 5)(2x - 1)(x - 3)$	4. i) $X =$ number of people who did not recover $H_0: p = 0.2, H_1: p \neq 0.2, \alpha = 5\%$ $X \sim B(30, 0.2)$ ii) $x \leq 1$ & $x \geq 12$ iii) Actual significance level 0.02 iv) No evidence to reject H_0, The new treatment is no different to the old one.
5. i) $f'(x) = 9x^2 - 8x - 8x^{-3} - 6x^{-4}$ ii) $\frac{3}{4}x^4 - \frac{4}{3}x^3 - 4x^{-1} - x^{-2} + c$	
6. Proof	
7. i) $19683 - 118098x + 314928x^2 - 489888x^3$ ii) 18533.0229	5. i) scatter graph ii) As the age increases, the height increases.
8. $21.49cm^2$	6. i) 98N ii) 32N
9. $30°, 150°, 199.5°, 340.5°$	7. i) $1.2ms^{-2}$ ii) 131.25m iii) 7.5s
10. $p \leq -\frac{8}{9}, p > 0$	8. i) 68.4m ii) 84.9m
11. Proof	
12. $x = 0.262 \ or \ x = -1$	9. i) $2.45ms^{-2}$ ii) 36.75N iii) 4.5m
13. i) $x(x - 4)^2$ ii) sketch iii) $k = 2 \ or - 2$	
14. i) $x = \ln 4$ ii) $x = 2e^3 + 1$	
15. i) $(-3, -9)$ ii) $15.75units^2$	
16. i) $C(5, -1)$ ii) $r = \sqrt{13}$ iii) $(x - 5)^2 + (y + 1)^2 = 13$	
17. i) proof ii) £198.12	

Paper E1	Paper E2
1. $32 - 80x + 80x^2$	1. i) Venn diagram
	ii) $\frac{1}{5}$
2. i) proof	
ii) $30°, 150°, 199.5°, 340.5°$	2. a) 0.1310
	b) Reject H_0, sufficient evidence to suggest the losses have increased.
3. i) (2,2)	
ii) $6y + x - 14 = 0$	3. i) 251.125
	ii) Median 87.9, IQR = 99.5
4. i) $\binom{6}{16}$	
ii) $\sqrt{73}$	4. i) 0.3
	ii) Venn Diagram
5. $x < -4, x > \frac{2}{3}$	iii) 0.7
	iv) 0.3
6. $-\frac{5}{3} < x < 2$	
	5. a) 36.9°
7. $x^4 - \frac{1}{8}x^{-2} + c$	b) 3.5N
8. i) proof	6. i) 17.1m
ii) $p \le 1 - 2\sqrt{15}, p \ge 1 + 2\sqrt{15}$	ii) 3.27s
iii) $\frac{1-2\sqrt{15}}{10}$	iii) 2.87s
9. i) proof	7. i) $1ms^{-2}$
ii) $3y + x - 20 = 0$	ii) 130m
iii) $\frac{20\sqrt{10}}{3}$	iii) 8.09s
10. i) $\log R = \log a + kt$	8. i) $-14ms^{-2}$
ii) graph	ii) 3.33s
iii) $R = 28.2(10^{0.09t})$	
iv) $R = 28.2$	
v) 2011	
11. i) $y + 3x - 15 = 0$	
ii) $B(0,15)$	
iii) $37.5units^2$	
12. $\frac{122}{3}$	
13. i) $C(4,1), r = \sqrt{34}$	
ii) $5y + 3x + 17 = 0$	
iii) $\frac{289}{30}units^2$	

Paper F1	Paper F2
1. i) $C(6,10), r = \sqrt{5}$ ii) $(x-6)^2 + (y-10)^2 = 5$ 2. i) $\frac{dy}{dx} = 12x^2 - 20x + 7$ ii) $\frac{dy}{dx} = -x^{-2} + 2x^{-3}$ iii) $\frac{dy}{dx} = 4x + 6 + 3x^{-2}$ 3. i) $-2 - 2\sqrt{2}$ ii) $8 + 3\sqrt{7}$ iii) $\frac{14+8\sqrt{3}}{3}$ 4. i) $x \geq -10$ ii) $-\frac{5}{3} \leq x < \frac{11}{3}$ iii) $x < -\frac{3}{2}$ & $x > 4$ 5. i) $8 - 12x + 6x^2 - x^3$ ii) $8 - 12y - 6y^2 + 11y^3 + 3y^4 - 3y^5 - y^6$ 6. $16y - 10x + 17 = 0$ 7. i) 82 ii) 13 iii) $\frac{157}{2}$ 8. $p < -1, p > 3$ 9. i) $(x+2)(x-4)(2x-1)$ ii) $x = -2, x = 4, x = \frac{1}{2}$ iii) sketch 10. i) proof ii) $887.8cm^2$ iii) show $\frac{d^2y}{dx^2} > 0$ iv) £10.65 11. $x = 1$ or -0.415 12. i) (3,78) & (4,77) ii) $72y + x + 216 = 0$	1. a) i) 0.1409 ii) 0.2288 iii) 0.4647 b) fixed number of trials, each trial has constant probability of success 2. i) 37.4 miles ii) 27.7 miles iii) 8.25 miles iv) 24.6 miles 3. i) tree diagram ii) 0.8 iii) 0.51 4. i) 11.76N ii) $t = 0.904s$ 5. a) $2ms^{-2}$ b) 12m 6. i) 23.5m ii) 3.72s iii) 2.63s 7. 9.6N

Printed in Great Britain
by Amazon

20409380R00068